Clydesdales AND Miniature Horses

Henry Thatcher

PowerKiDS press.

New York

Published in 2014 by The Rosen Publishing Group, Inc.
29 East 21st Street, New York, NY 10010

First Edition

Produced for Rosen by Cyan Candy, LLC
Editor: Joshua Shadowens
Designer: Erica Clendening, Cyan Candy

Photo Credits: Cover (top), pp. 5, 6, 8, 10, 15, 16, 18, 21, 27, 30 Shutterstock.com; cover (bottom)
© Laurie Stamm; pp. 4, 13, 25, 31 © Pete Markham, via Wikimedia Commons; pp. 7, 12, 17, 22, 24,
28, 23 © B. Garrett; p. 9 © Derrick Coetzee; p. 11 Photomaggie, via Wikimdedia Commons; p. 14 Bob
MacInnes, via Wikimedia Commons; p. 20 John Braid/Shutterstock.com; p. 26 James Emery, via
Wikimedia Commons.

Library of Congress Cataloging-in-Publication Data

Thatcher, Henry.
 Clydesdales and miniature horses / by Henry Thatcher. — First edition.
    pages cm. — (Big animals, small animals)
 Includes index.
 ISBN 978-1-4777-6102-1 (library) — ISBN 978-1-4777-6103-8 (pbk.) —
 ISBN 978-1-4777-6104-5 (6-pack)
 1. Clydesdale horse—Juvenile literature. 2. Miniature horses—Juvenile literature. 3. Horses—
Juvenile literature. I. Title.
 SF293T43 2014
 636.1'5—dc23

                          2013026020

Manufactured in the United States of America

CPSIA Compliance Information: Batch #W14PK2: For Further Information contact Rosen Publishing, New York, New York at 1-800-237-9932

Table of Contents

Horses Big AND Small

Horses have been used to do many jobs for people for thousands of years. While there is only one species of horse, there are around 400 different **breeds**. Some horse breeds were bred to be strong. Others are bred for speed. Some

Here, a miniature horse walks beside a normal-sized horse. As you can see, their heights are quite different!

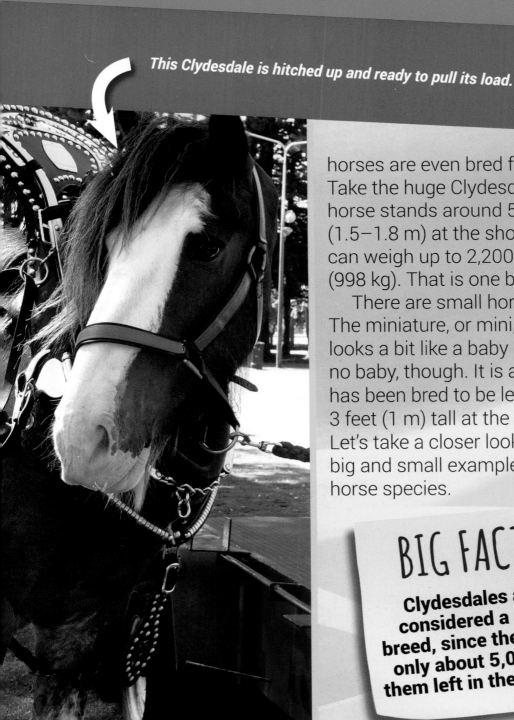

horses are even bred for size. Take the huge Clydesdale. This horse stands around 5 to 6 feet (1.5–1.8 m) at the shoulder and can weigh up to 2,200 pounds (998 kg). That is one big animal!

There are small horses, too. The miniature, or mini, horse looks a bit like a baby horse. It is no baby, though. It is a horse that has been bred to be less than 3 feet (1 m) tall at the shoulder. Let's take a closer look at these big and small examples of the horse species.

BIG FACT!

Clydesdales are considered a rare breed, since there are only about 5,000 of them left in the world.

Where IN THE World?

Clydesdales first were bred in Clydesdale, Scotland, which is where they got their name. Horses from Belgium were brought to Scotland and bred with the Scottish farm horses. At first, Clydesdales were not as tall as they are today. They were strong, though, and used as **draft** horses and worked on farms. Over time, they were bred to be taller, and the present-day Clydesdale breed was born. They were first called Clydesdales in 1826.

As you can see, the miniature horse isn't much larger than a dog or a cat. ▶

By 1830, people were buying Clydesdales in England. In the 1900s, Clydesdales were exported to other places, including the Americas, New Zealand, and Australia.

Mini horses are thought to have been first bred in the 1600s in England. Today, they are bred in places around the world, including the United States, Argentina, and South Africa.

Horses at Home

Horses are classified as livestock. This means they live on farms and are raised to provide food, **fiber**, or labor. There are few wild breeds of horses. Most are **domesticated** like the Clydesdale and mini horse.

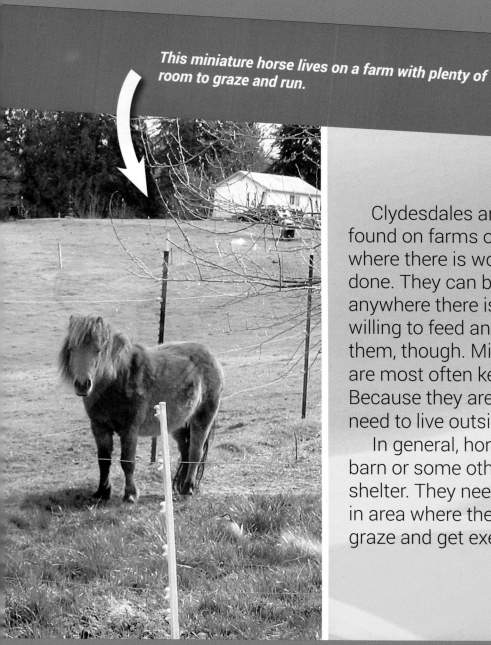

This miniature horse lives on a farm with plenty of room to graze and run.

Clydesdales are often found on farms or places where there is work to be done. They can be found anywhere there is a person willing to feed and shelter them, though. Mini horses are most often kept as pets. Because they are horses, they need to live outside.

In general, horses need a barn or some other kind of shelter. They need a fenced in area where they can safely graze and get exercise.

Clydesdales are large animals that can be extremely helpful with dragging heavy farming equipment and other big items, such as carts or carriages.

Horses need plenty of clean, fresh water and lots of hay or grass to feed on. They drink up to 12 gallons (45 l) of water per day. They also eat about 2.5 percent of their body weight. Considering horses like the Clydesdale can weigh up to 2,200 pounds (998 kg), that is a lot of food!

Miniature horses are mostly kept as pets. The women are using halters and lead ropes. These are used to train the horse at a basic level. ▶

Here, three beautiful Clydesdale horses hover together in their corral. They are most likely waiting for their food.

BIG FACT!

The only living wild horse is Przewalski's horse. This horse lives on the steppes, or rocky hillsides, of Asia, especially in Mongolia.

Horses, big and small, need a home where they receive regular brushing of their coats, tails, and manes. Their hooves must be cared for and shoed by a **farrier**. If they become sick they need veterinary care, too.

Are They Alike?

Clydesdales and mini horses could not be more different in size. However, in most other ways they are very much the same. They are both in the genus *Equus*, which has two subspecies *Equus ferus* and *Equus ferus caballus*. *Equus ferus caballus* includes all domesticated horses, including Clydesdales and mini horses.

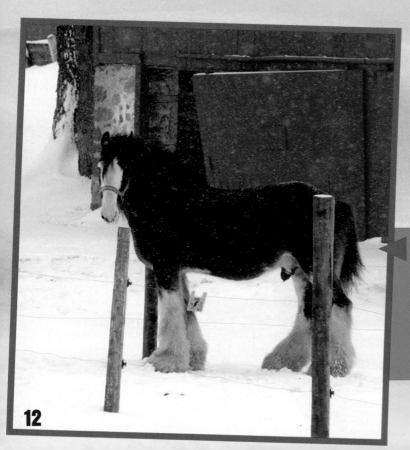

Here, a young Clydesdale horse is baring a snowstorm. Its thick fur, especially around its feet, keep it warm.

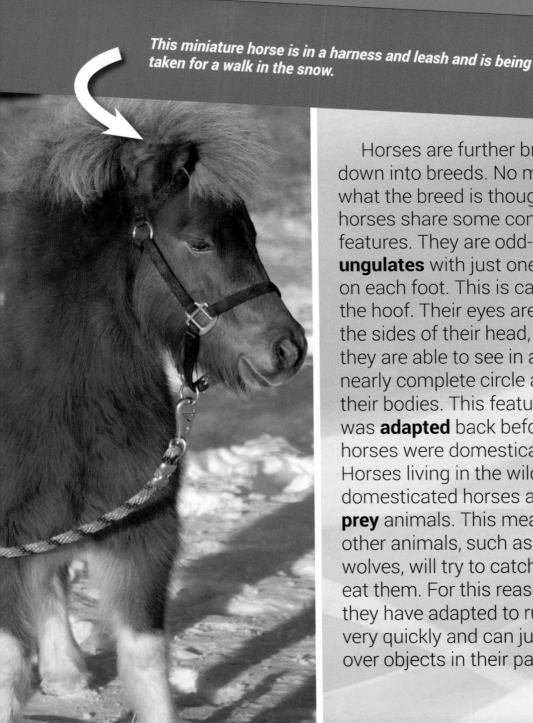

This miniature horse is in a harness and leash and is being taken for a walk in the snow.

Horses are further broken down into breeds. No matter what the breed is though, all horses share some common features. They are odd-toed **ungulates** with just one toe on each foot. This is called the hoof. Their eyes are on the sides of their head, and they are able to see in a nearly complete circle around their bodies. This feature was **adapted** back before horses were domesticated. Horses living in the wild and domesticated horses are **prey** animals. This means other animals, such as wolves, will try to catch and eat them. For this reason, they have adapted to run very quickly and can jump over objects in their path.

A Clydesdale mare and her foal are standing close together in a field. Horse mothers are very protective of their young.

They can also sleep standing up. This allows them to escape quickly should a **predator** be nearby.

Mother horses carry their babies for about 11 months. When the baby horses, or foals, are born they are able to walk and run right away. This is another defense against predators. Horses can live to be between 25 and 35 years old.

Comparing CLYDESDALES

Size .... Around 6 feet (1.8 m) at the shoulder

Habitat............... domesticated; lives with people

Diet.................... herbivore; mainly grasses and grains

Predators .... big cats and wolves

Prey .... none

Life Span............ 25 to 30 years

AND MINIATURE HORSES

Size .... Under 3 feet (1 m) at the shoulder

Habitat .... domesticated; lives with people

Diet .... herbivore; mainly grasses and grains

Predators .... big cats, wolves, and coyotes

Prey.................... none

Life Span............ 25 to 35 years

One Big Horse!

Clydesdales have been bred to be big. If you have ever seen one of these horses in a parade you know that the breeding plan worked! Clydesdales have huge, strong bodies and thick, sturdy legs. They are known for the white "feathering" of the fur around their feet. Often the bottom part of their legs is white, though sometimes not all four legs are white. Clydesdales often have a white blaze on their faces and black manes and tails. The most common coat color is bay, which is a reddish-brown color. They can also have chestnut, black, gray, or roan coats. A roan coat is one in which there are a lot of white hairs mixed in with the other color.

As draft horses, Clydesdales are built for pulling heavy loads, such as plows, carriages, or carts. They are often used for farm work, but have also been used to haul loads in mines. They are also used in logging or to do work in places where it would be hard for machines or trucks to reach. Clydesdales were often used as warhorses during World War I.

Two Clydesdales are harnessed side by side to pull an extra heavy load.

BIG FACT!

Clydesdale horseshoes are about 20 inches (50 cm) long, from end to end, and weigh about 5 pounds (2.3 kg).

Today they are still used for many of these reasons. They are also often used as drum horses and march in many parades.

Mini BUT Mighty

Some people look at mini horses and think they are ponies. While it is true that they are small like ponies, they are built like horses. Ponies tend to have thicker legs and broader bodies and faces. Mini horses look like miniature versions of larger horses.

The smallest mini horse is the Falabella. It tends to be between 28 and 34 inches (0.7–0.8 m) tall. This breed looks like a miniature racehorse. It has a slim build and is meant for speed, not pulling. There are many mini horses that can pull, though. Mini horses are too small for riders, except for small children. Yet they can pull one or two people in a wagon.

Miniature horses come in a wide variety of colors and patterns.

Some people use mini horses as guide animals for blind people. These horses must be calm, gentle, and smart. The horse goes through lots of training and tests. If they are ready, they go to live in a person's home and help them with their daily tasks. Most mini horses prefer to live outside, though.

This is a close-up of a miniature horse. They have thick fur to protect them in cold weather since most horses lives outside.

Baby mini horses, or foals, are generally around 1 to 2 feet (0.3–0.6 m) tall when they are born. They reach their full height by the time they are 3 years old. Like all horses, mini horse foals are able to get up and walk very soon after birth.

Diets: Big AND Small

Have you ever heard someone say that a person eats like a horse? They may have been thinking of a Clydesdale. In one day, a Clydesdale can eat up to 25 quarts (24 l) of grain and 60 pounds (27 kg) of hay, plus drink 30 gallons (114 l) of water!

Miniature horses do not eat quite as much as Clydesdales. However, even though they seem small compared to Clydesdales, they are still large animals that eat a lot of food.

All horses like to eat grasses and grains. If there is not a lot of fresh grass available, a horse can be given hay. Hay is dried grass. Horses also need salt and other trace minerals. These can be bought in the form of a brick.

A child reaches out to feed a miniature horse at a petting zoo.

Horses use the spit, or saliva, in their mouth to help them digest their diet of grains and grasses. They produce up to 10 gallons (38 l) of saliva per day!

Carrots and apples are okay to feed as a sweet treat, but should be fed in small amounts. You also need to make sure your Clydesdale or mini horse does not eat too much fresh grass.

Horses that are eating lots of hay or other dry matter need a lot of water. When they are grazing on fresh grasses they drink less water.

In general, plants are hard to break down. Many animals that graze on grasses have many stomachs to help break down the tough plant matter. Some chew, swallow, and bring the grasses back into their mouths. Horses do not do this. They have special **organisms** living in their stomachs that help them digest their meals.

Miniature horses munch on grass in their paddock on a farm.

Big or Small, Does it Matter?

Clydesdales are big, powerful animals. They are an impressive sight if you ever get a chance to see one. They are hardworking horses, too. Mini horses are a lot smaller, but they are still beautiful and strong. Clydesdales need more food, water, and space than do mini horses.

A miniature horse gets to know a young goat through a fence on a farm.

They are both horse breeds, though, and they have similar needs for shelter and diet. Both also need to see a vet at least once a year, and have their hooves cared for by the farrier.

In the end, how big these animals are does not really matter. They are both wonderful examples of horses, big and small.

 A woman shows a Clydesdale at a fall agricultural fair.

Glossary

adapted (uh-DAP-ted) Changed to fit requirements.
breeds (BREEDZ) Groups of animals that look alike and have the same relatives.
domesticated (duh-MES-tih-kayt-id) Raised to live with people.
draft (DRAFT) Used for pulling loads.
farrier (FER-ee-er) A special kind of blacksmith who makes horseshoes and trims and cares for horses' hooves.
fiber (FY-ber) Parts in food from plants that the body cannot break down but that help the body get rid of waste.
organisms (OR-guh-nih-zumz) Living beings made of dependent parts.
predator (PREH-duh-ter) An animal that kills other animals for food.
prey (PRAY) An animal that is hunted by another animal for food.
ungulates (UNG-gyuh-luts) Animals with hooves.

Index

Websites

Due to the changing nature of Internet links, PowerKids Press has developed an online list of websites related to the subject of this book. This site is updated regularly. Please use this link to access the list: www.powerkids.com/basa/horse/